DARINGWOMEN

25 WOMEN WHO RULED

Rebecca Stanborough

D0335993

Raintree is an imprint of Capstone Global Library Limited, a company incorporated in England and Wales having its registered office at 264 Banbury Road, Oxford, OX2 7DY – Registered company number: 6695582

www.raintree.co.uk
myorders@raintree.co.uk

Text © Capstone Global Library Limited 2019
The moral rights of the proprietor have been asserted.

All rights reserved. No part of this publication may be reproduced in any form or by any means (including photocopying or storing it in any medium by electronic means and whether or not transiently or incidentally to some other use of this publication) without the written permission of the copyright owner, except in accordance with the provisions of the Copyright, Designs and Patents Act 1988 or under the terms of a licence issued by the Copyright Licensing Agency, Barnard's Inn, 86 Fetter Lane, London, EC4A 1EN (www.cla.co.uk). Applications for the copyright owner's written permission should be addressed to the publisher.

Edited by Anna Butzer
Designed by Russell Griesmer
Original illustrations © Capstone Global Library Limited 2019
Picture research by Svetlana Zhurkin
Production by Laura Manthe
Originated by Capstone Global Library Ltd
Printed and bound in India

ISBN 978 1 4747 6252 6 (hardback)   ISBN 978 1 4747 6256 4 (paperback)
22 21 20 19 18   23 22 21 20 19
10 9 8 7 6 5 4 3 2 1   10 9 8 7 6 5 4 3 2 1

British Library Cataloguing in Publication Data
A full catalogue record for this book is available from the British Library.

Acknowledgements
We would like to thank the following for permission to reproduce photographs: AP Photo: David Guttenfelder, cover; Capstone Press: 18, 27, 37; Dreamstime: Laurence Agron, 51; Getty Images: AFP/Aamir Qureshi, 14, Bettmann, 55, Robert R. McElroy, 39, The LIFE Images Collection/Bob Peterson, 23; Library of Congress, 29; Newscom: akg-images, 11, Icon Sportswire/John Korduner, 49, MCT/Abaca Press/Olivier Douliery, 21, Polaris/Baldev Kapoor, 17, Polaris/i-Images/Dinendra Haria, 25, Reuters/Ivan Alvarado, 19, Reuters/Lucas Jackson, 35, Reuters/Philippe Wojazer, 33, Reuters/Stephen Lam, 36, Sipa/Romuald Meigneux, 31, Zuma Press/Christy Bowe, 53; Shutterstock: 360b, 9, Andrea Delbo, 44, Banana Oil, 4–5, DFree, 46, Jaguar PS, 41, Leonard Zhukovsky, 57, Shaun Jeffers, 7, Twocoms, 43; Wikimedia: Margaret Thatcher Foundation/Chris Collins, 12

Design Elements by Shutterstock

Every effort has been made to contact copyright holders of material reproduced in this book. Any omissions will be rectified in subsequent printings if notice is given to the publisher.

All the internet addresses (URLs) given in this book were valid at the time of going to press. However, due to the dynamic nature of the internet, some addresses may have changed, or sites may have changed or ceased to exist since publication. While the author and publisher regret any inconvenience this may cause readers, no responsibility for any such changes can be accepted by either the author or the publisher.

CONTENTS

INTRODUCTION

Women have led nations, fought for freedom, created great works of art, built companies, smashed records, opened doors of opportunity and inspired millions of people. Some were born into powerful families and inherited great wealth. Some knew what it was like to be hungry or homeless. Every one of them worked hard to achieve her dreams. Every one of them changed the world.

Women throughout history have changed the world.

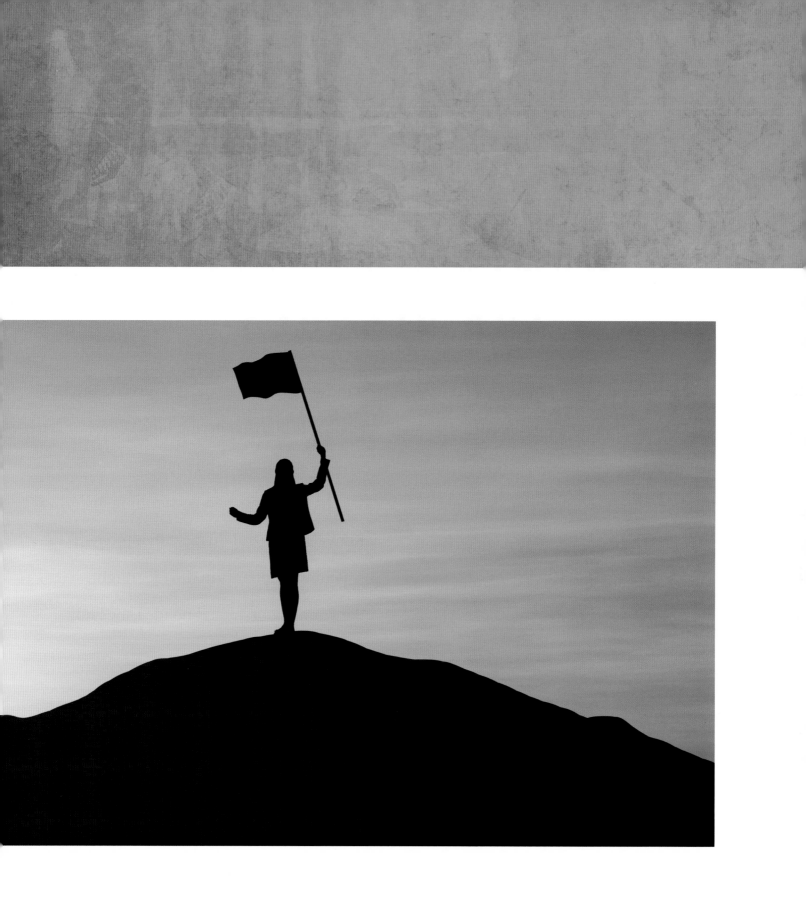

Chapter 1

WOMEN WHO RULED FOR DECADES

Few people can imagine what it is like to be responsible for the welfare of an entire country. These women didn't have to imagine it. They ruled nations. They appointed cabinets, negotiated with foreign diplomats, started and ended wars and made daily decisions that changed the lives of millions. These women rocked the world.

Queen Elizabeth II
(b. 1926)

Princess Elizabeth was awake in the early morning hours. She stood at the window of the treehouse, watching the elephants at the watering hole below.

"They're pink," she said.

The elephants had been rolling in Kenya's colourful dust. At that moment, watching elephants in the moonlight, the young woman had no idea she had become queen.

She would assume the tremendous responsibility the next day, when she learned that her beloved father, King George VI, had died. In the 65 years since then, Queen Elizabeth II has steadied the nation in an

Queen Elizabeth II, 2012

era of great change. During her reign, more than 40 colonies have gained independence to form new nations. She has worked with 13 different prime ministers and countless other politicians with widely varying political views. She has been on 271 visits to 128 nations around the world.

What has remained constant throughout her reign is her commitment to duty and service. She begins nearly every day with a review of her famous red boxes, which contain reports on the actions of Parliament, important letters and government documents.

Her schedule remains challenging. She meets people from all over the world almost every day. She lends her support to charities and attends all sorts of different events. And while some of these duties may seem merely ceremonial, her participation in the life of the nation unifies an increasing population.

As the UK's longest-reigning monarch, she has received her share of criticism. But she is almost universally admired for her dedication to serving her people and country.

Angela Merkel
(b. 1954)
Chancellor of Germany

Angela Merkel grew up in a divided nation surrounded by walls. West Germany was a free, democratic society. But in East Germany, where Angela Merkel and her family lived, a strict communist government controlled jobs, housing and education. Those who disagreed with the government found themselves out of a job, cut off from schooling or imprisoned.

Angela Merkel's father was a Lutheran pastor in an atheist nation, and her family was under constant surveillance. A 165-kilometre (103-mile) concrete wall through Berlin separated east from west Germany. In the wall's 28-year history, nearly 200 people were killed trying to cross the wall. Germany was reunited as a democratic nation in 1990. But growing up in a family whose values clashed with the government may have given Merkel a lasting gift. She developed an ability to cautiously consider all solutions to a problem before deciding what to do. Or perhaps being analytical was simply her nature: She was trained as a mathematician and physicist.

Angela Merkel was elected the first female chancellor of Germany in 2005, and is still chancellor today. She has guided Germany through two serious crises. The first was the economic crash that struck Europe in 2008. Merkel's carefully considered policies made Germany the strongest economy in Europe at a time when some other nations buckled.

Angela Merkel at a press conference after a meeting with the NATO Secretary General in the Federal Chancellery in Berlin, June 2016

In 2015 and 2016, disasters in Syria and Libya caused millions to flee their homelands in the largest human migration in modern history. Under Merkel's leadership, Germany opened its doors to the refugees. Speaking of these refugees, Merkel said, "[I]t is not masses that arrive but individuals. For every human being has the dignity which is given to him by God."

Indira Gandhi
(1917–1984)
Prime Minister of India

Indira Gandhi grew up in a family of daring activists. During India's quest for independence from British rule, her family members were imprisoned many times. She was so accustomed to hearing about protests that she made them part of her childhood games. She would set up two groups of dolls, freedom fighters and police, and enact confrontations between them. Later, this became reality. She was imprisoned for speaking out against the British Raj, the British rulers of India, when she was 24 years old.

India gained independence in 1947. Gandhi's father, Jawaharlal Nehru, was elected prime minister. She shadowed him as he met with world leaders and made decisions about India's future. It was excellent training. In 1966 Gandhi was elected the first female prime minister of India, the largest democracy in the world.

In the years that followed, the people of India alternately adored and hated Gandhi. They loved her for skilfully executing a 14-day war to free neighbouring Bangladesh from Pakistani rule. But later she was hated with equal strength.

Gandhi's government was accused of corruption. Some officials took huge bribes for favours. Drought brought hunger, and people felt she didn't do enough to help. When a court ruled that Gandhi had rigged an election, she declared a state of emergency instead of leaving office. She had her opponents arrested. She suspended rights such as freedom of speech and freedom of the press. When she finally allowed another election, she lost.

Countless Berliners greeted Indira Gandhi during her visit to East Berlin in 1976.

Years later she was elected prime minister again. The people of India forgave Gandhi's earlier failures. But there was one group of people she had deeply offended. India's Punjab state was home to many people in the Sikh religion. Some Sikhs wanted to separate and form their own nation. Gandhi wanted India to remain united. In June 1984 she ordered the army to raid the Golden Temple in Amritsar, the most important Sikh temple. The soldiers killed hundreds of people and nearly destroyed the holy place.

In revenge, two of Gandhi's Sikh bodyguards assassinated her. She was mourned by millions, and is remembered for both the heights and depths she reached as a leader.

Margaret Thatcher, 1989

Margaret Thatcher
(1925–2013)
Prime Minister of the UK

The 24-year-old candidate stepped onto the soapbox, looking somewhat out of place among the bricklayers of Dartford. The crowd paid attention – whether because of her fierce speech or from the novelty of seeing a female candidate. Margaret Roberts was in her element. She had been listening to political debates since her childhood. Though she had studied chemistry at Oxford University, it was politics that thrilled her.

When Margaret Thatcher took office as prime minister in 1979, the UK was still reeling from a period of economic trouble known as the "Winter of Discontent". Inflation was at a staggering 10 per cent, making it hard for ordinary people to afford the necessities of life. Over 1 million people were out of work, and some trade unions had gone on strike. Even gravediggers and dustmen were refusing to work until their demands were met.

Thatcher was a lifelong conservative. She and the Conservative Party believed that it was a mistake for people to depend on the government for financial help. Conservatives also believed that government needed to be small to make room for private companies to grow and employ more people. At first, conservative policies led to a deeper recession, and Thatcher's popularity wavered.

But the economy eventually rebounded, and Thatcher's sharp reduction in government spending and tight rein on unions became more appreciated. When the UK went to war with Argentina to protect the Falkland Islands – a British territory – her popularity rose even further. A Soviet diplomat once called her the "Iron Lady", and the nickname stuck.

Though she eventually resigned her position in the face of opposition during her third term, she was the longest-serving British prime minister in the 20th century. She served in the House of Lords until her death at the age of 87.

> *Don't follow the crowd, let the crowd follow you.*
> —Margaret Thatcher

Benazir Bhutto waved to her supporters during a rally in the port city of Karachi, Pakistan, February 1999.

Benazir Bhutto
(1953–2007)
Prime Minister of Pakistan

Prime Minister Benazir Bhutto stood on a glacier in Siachen, the highest point in Pakistan, listening to a military briefing. She was surrounded by snowy peaks – and the Indian army was encamped just across the Gyong La Pass. In this, the world's highest battleground, the prime minister was keeping a secret. She was going to have a baby.

Weeks later, when news got out, Bhutto found herself on a different kind of battlefield. Some people argued that she couldn't lead the country while she was pregnant. She gave birth to her child and returned to work the next day.

Bhutto was the first democratically elected female prime minister of a Muslim nation. Her father, Prime Minister Zulfikar Ali Bhutto, had helped modernize Pakistan, opening up opportunities for women and minorities. His progressive ideas did not sit well with everyone, however. When Bhutto was a young woman, her father was assassinated.

For the next decade, Bhutto and thousands of other Pakistanis were imprisoned for opposing the government.

Many were tortured and killed. Despite years of imprisonment, she did not give in to those who demanded that she withdraw from public service.

In 1988 when elections were finally permitted again, Bhutto won by a landslide. Immediately, she began working towards democracy. She lifted the ban on labour unions. She restored freedom of the press and freed political prisoners. Her government brought electricity, clean water and phone services to remote villages. She even reached out to build peace with India. She was elected to a second term as prime minister in 1993.

Sadly, not everyone supported the democratic changes she had made. In December 2007, Bhutto was killed in a bomb attack while campaigning for a third term.

Bhutto's trip to the disputed Siachen glacier was symbolic of her life. She climbed to spectacular heights. She walked into dangerous territory in her quest for peace. And she listened patiently to the advice of others, knowing all the while that she had to rely on the strength she had within herself.

ICELAND IS CLOSING THE GENDER GAP!

The tiny nation of Iceland has a population of around 330,000 people – and it is a great place to be a woman. In 1980 Vigdís Finnbogadóttir became the first woman in the world to be elected head of state. She served as president until 1996. From 2009 to 2012 Iceland had a female prime minister, Jóhanna Sigurðardóttir. And in 2016 Iceland elected a record number of women to Parliament: 30 of its 63 members. For the past nine years, Iceland's gender equality has been ranked number one in the world by the World Economic Forum.

Chapter 2

WOMEN WHO RULED IN POLITICS

What does it take to represent a nation? In democratic countries, it takes the confidence of the people. Each one of these women knew what it was to win the votes of her fellow citizens. And each entered a field dominated by male leaders who were not accustomed to women in positions of power. These women broke new ground, showing people what it's like when women run the world.

Ellen Johnson Sirleaf
(b. 1938)
President of Liberia

The African nation of Liberia is full of dramatic differences: coastal cities and dense rainforests, indigenous African people and descendants of American slaves, valuable natural resources and human poverty. Few leaders could unite a country as divided as Liberia has been. But as the first democratically

Ellen Johnson Sirleaf, 2013

elected female head of state in all of Africa, President Ellen Johnson Sirleaf has proved her skill in bringing Liberia's people together.

As a girl, Sirleaf watched both of her parents become leaders in a diverse community. Her father was a lawyer and member of the legislature. Her mother was, for a time, a travelling minister. Sirleaf's family dined with President Hilary Johnson, Liberia's first native-born president. But they also ate with villagers in remote parts of the country.

Sirleaf married and had children early. But unlike many women of her era, she also pursued her education. She travelled to the United States and studied to become an accountant and, later on, an economist. When she returned to Liberia, she worked in the Treasury Department. She

YEARS SERVED BY FEMALE HEADS OF STATE OR GOVERNMENT, 1964–2017

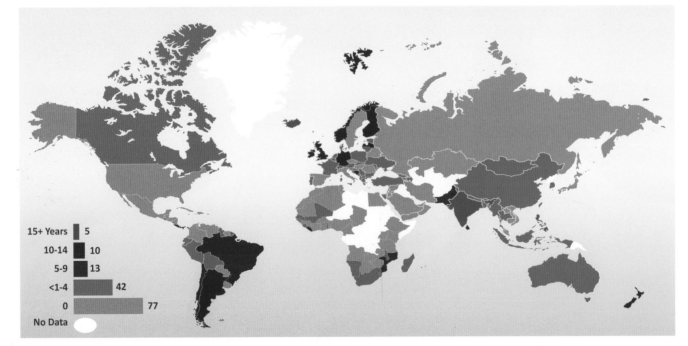

15+ Years	5
10-14	10
5-9	13
<1-4	42
0	77
No Data	

Most of the world's nations have never had a female leader.

bravely criticized policies that kept Liberia poor and underdeveloped.

In 1980 the president of Liberia, William Tolbert, was assassinated. The military staged a coup, taking over the government. Sirleaf was imprisoned and narrowly escaped death. She fled the country, but continued to work for the benefit of Liberia and other African nations in the United Nations Development Programme.

Years of intense civil war followed. Then, in 2005, a free election took place, and Sirleaf became president. In her two terms, she drastically reduced Liberia's national debt. She worked to heal the war-torn nation. In 2011 Sirleaf was awarded the Nobel Peace Prize for her work in improving the lives of women.

Michelle Bachelet announcing her cabinet members before taking office as Chile's new president, January 2014

Michelle Bachelet
(b. 1951)
President of Chile

In the dark hours of 11 September 1973, soldiers under the command of Chilean dictator Augusto Pinochet raided the home of well-known Air Force General Alberto Bachelet. For the next several months, they questioned and tortured him, finally releasing him several months later. Weakened by the abuse, General Bachelet's heart gave out. Like thousands of other victims of Pinochet's rule, he died in custody. Not long afterwards, Pinochet's soldiers arrested and interrogated General Bachelet's wife and daughter, and then forced them into exile.

The interrogators could not have known that Michelle Bachelet, the daughter of the deceased general, would one day become Chile's first woman president.

Michelle Bachelet returned to Chile as a paediatrician. She specialized in treating the children of those who had disappeared under Pinochet's rule. When Pinochet was ousted in 1973, Bachelet continued working to heal the country he had torn apart.

In 2000 President Ricardo Lagos appointed her Minister of Health. She worked to create a health system that guaranteed health care for everyone, including the poor. In two years, she reduced the waiting list for doctors' appointments by 82 per cent.

Because of Bachelet's success in changing the health system, Lagos appointed her Minister of Defence. She was the first woman in Latin America to hold such a position in the military. But her new role brought her face to face with people from her past. She was once in the same lift as the man who had ordered her tortured when she was being held by Pinochet.

She made an important decision. She would not seek revenge. She later told reporters that Chileans might never agree about what had happened in their past, but they all had to work together to create a better future. As Minister of Defence, she reformed the way the military interacted with the public. Instead of being used to oppress people, the military was now seen as a force for good, rescuing victims of floods and earthquakes, for example.

In 2006 the people of Chile elected Bachelet president. She served two terms: 2006 to 2010 and 2014 to 2017. During her presidency, she appointed the same number of female cabinet members as males. She helped enact laws that guaranteed equal wages for male and female employees. She expanded free education. And she worked to protect Chile's environment, building South America's first geothermal energy plant and creating a 460,272-square-kilometre (286,000-square-mile) marine reserve around Easter Island.

Madeleine Albright
(b. 1937)
US Secretary of State

Imagine a train late at night, carrying two parents with two suitcases, hastily packed. With them is one small child. It is a story that played out thousands of times

Madeleine Albright was awarded the Presidential Medal of Freedom by US President Barack Obama at the White House, May 2012.

during the early years of World War II. In this story, the little girl – Marie – would grow up in the United States. She would devote her life to preserving democracies all over the world.

Madeleine Albright was born Marie Jana Korbel in Czechoslovakia in 1937. When she was two years old, Nazi soldiers invaded her country. She and her parents fled. Almost every member of her family who stayed in Czechoslovakia died in concentration camps.

For many years, Albright's life followed the pattern customary for young women of her era: high school, university, then marriage and family. But Madeleine wanted more. In an early essay, she wrote "somehow it must be possible to be a responsible mother, a good wife and have an intellectually satisfying job".

Albright found that satisfying job in international politics. She went to work first for Maine Senator Edmund Muskie while earning her PhD from Columbia University. After she had earned her degree, Albright worked as an adviser to the National Security Council. In 1993 President Bill Clinton appointed her US ambassador to the United Nations. She was often surrounded by male leaders while she worked there. She helped other leaders strengthen democracy in nations, including the Balkan countries of Eastern Europe.

In 1996 Albright was unanimously confirmed as US Secretary of State, the highest-ranking woman in the nation's history. She helped strengthen democracy in countries that were once part of the communist Soviet Union, including Czechoslovakia. She participated in groundbreaking efforts to secure peace in the Middle East. She was the first secretary of state ever to meet with the leader of North Korea.

Madeleine Albright, a one-time refugee, dedicated her life to securing democracy worldwide. US President Barack Obama awarded her the Presidential Medal of Freedom in 2012.

Shirley Chisholm
(1924–2005)
US Representative

When Shirley Chisholm stepped up to the podium in 1972 to announce that she was running for the US presidency, she had already earned the support of thousands of Americans. Four years earlier, she had been elected to the US House of Representatives. She was the first African-American woman ever elected to US Congress.

Standing behind the bristling microphones that day in 1972, Shirley

Shirley Chisholm, 1970

Chisholm said, "I am not the candidate of black America, though I am black and proud. I am not the candidate of the women's movement of this country, though I am a woman and equally proud of that. I am not the candidate of any political bosses or special interests. I am the people's candidate."

Chisholm learned to fight for the interests of people in New York's neighbourhoods, where she witnessed discrimination of all kinds. As a member of the New York State Assembly from 1964–1968, she rallied against unfair housing practices that left African Americans, Puerto Ricans, Jewish people and poor people with few choices other than crowded tenements and public housing projects. She successfully sponsored laws that made unemployment benefits available to domestic workers. She championed the SEEK programme, which enabled disadvantaged students to succeed at university.

When she was elected to Congress in 1968, Chisholm was initially assigned to the House Agriculture Committee. In a shocking move for a newly elected representative, she demanded to be reassigned to a different committee – one where she could fight for the needs of her community. It worked. Challenging her assignment was just the first battle Chisholm fought. Sponsoring more than 50 pieces of legislation, she earned the nickname "fighting Shirley". She helped expand the food stamp programme and start other programmes that helped families feed their children. She made sure minimum wage was applied to domestic workers. And she fought to end US involvement in the Vietnam War.

Chisholm did not win the Democratic nomination in the 1972

presidential race. Most people believe that she never intended to win. She ran to awaken Americans to the possibility of an African-American president, and a female one.

She once told reporters, "My greatest political asset, which professional politicians fear, is my mouth . . ." She left Congress after seven terms in office and began travelling the US teaching and giving lectures. For the rest of her life, she challenged people to change US systems so that everyone would benefit from them.

Brenda Hale, DBE

(b. 1945)

President of the Supreme Court of the UK

Brenda Hale studied law at Cambridge University, where she experienced what it was like to be

Brenda Hale, 2017

outnumbered. Of the 100 students studying law, just 6 were female. Being one of just a few women may have been excellent training for her work in the British judiciary, where women make up just a tiny percentage of judges. After she graduated, she began teaching law at Manchester University. During her 18-year career as a professor, she wrote a book that explored how British law had treated women through the ages.

In 1984 Hale became the first woman appointed to the Law Commission, an organization that reforms outdated laws. She helped to modernize family law with the Children's Act of 1989. The new law made it clear how parents, the government, courts and agencies should interact to protect children. She also helped change laws on divorce and mental health care.

In 2009 Hale became the first woman ever appointed to the Supreme Court of the United Kingdom. Hale was named its president in 2017. That same year, a second female justice, Jill Black, was appointed to the Supreme Court.

Baroness Hale continues to press for greater diversity in the British judiciary. She told a group of female judges that a diverse court would enable people to "feel that the courts are their courts; that their cases are being decided and the law is being made by people like them."

The purpose of any human rights protection is to protect the rights of those whom the majority are unwilling to protect ...
—Brenda Hale

WOMEN ON THE US SUPREME COURT

Justice Sandra Day O'Connor was the first woman appointed to the US Supreme Court. She served from 1981 until she retired in 2006. She was awarded the US Presidential Medal of Freedom, the nation's highest civilian honour, by President Barack Obama in 2009. Today, three women serve as associate justices on the US Supreme Court. Justice Ruth Bader Ginsburg was appointed in 1993, Justice Sonia Sotomayor was appointed in 2009 and Justice Elena Kagan was appointed in 2010.

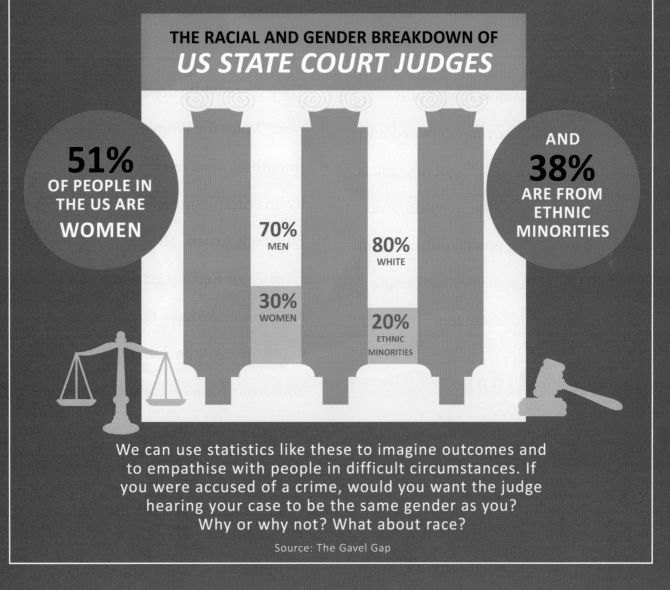

THE RACIAL AND GENDER BREAKDOWN OF
US STATE COURT JUDGES

51%
OF PEOPLE IN THE US ARE
WOMEN

70%
MEN

30%
WOMEN

80%
WHITE

20%
ETHNIC MINORITIES

AND
38%
ARE FROM ETHNIC MINORITIES

We can use statistics like these to imagine outcomes and to empathise with people in difficult circumstances. If you were accused of a crime, would you want the judge hearing your case to be the same gender as you? Why or why not? What about race?

Source: The Gavel Gap

a job at a beauty salon. That's where fortune turned its face towards her.

In 1910 Arden borrowed a small sum of money from her brother and opened her own beauty salon. She began creating her own line of beauty products. Inside the salon, clients received expensive facial treatments, massages, hair styling and makeovers in a lavish spa environment. Before Elizabeth Arden had entered the market, make-up was considered almost taboo in the United States. It was worn by stage actresses and film stars. Arden made it acceptable – even glamorous – for everyone.

Elizabeth Arden had a special knack for marketing. During the Great Depression, when thousands of companies folded, Elizabeth Arden succeeded. The company made a profit of $4 million during the 1930s. During World War II she gave her lipsticks special names such as "Victory Red", which made wearing them seem patriotic.

Elizabeth Arden was a fearsome boss. She paid her employees well but insisted that they work as hard as she did. She was also an innovator: her company was the first to offer travel sizes, first to send women door to door to demonstrate products and first to incorporate the founder's name into the product line.

More than 100 years have passed since Elizabeth Arden distributed lipstick to New York City's suffragettes. Today, there are Red Door Spas worldwide, and the company generates revenues of $966 million a year.

Ursula Burns
(b. 1958)
First Female Chief Executive Officer (CEO) of a Fortune 500 Company

Ursula Burns grew up in the Baruch Houses – public housing on New York City's Delancey Street. At the time, the area was populated by African American, Jewish and Hispanic families – almost all of them poor. Burns' mother ran a childcare business in her home. To bring in extra money, she ironed other people's clothes. Though she struggled at times to keep everyone fed, Burns' mother managed to send her three children to a fee-paying Catholic school. Ursula excelled at maths.

"Many people told me I had three strikes against me," Burns said. "I was black. I was a girl. And I was poor."

The accepted path for Burns would have been to become a nurse or a teacher. But Burns longed to be an engineer. She graduated from the New York Polytechnic Institute in 1980 and from New York's Columbia University in 1981. Then she got an internship at Xerox, a company well known for its copier machines. That internship led to a job.

Ursula Burns, 2014

One day early in her career, Burns did something that showed Xerox executives what a strong leader she would become. In a large meeting, someone asked the vice president why Xerox was so focused on hiring women and ethnic minorities. Burns thought the vice president should not have dignified the question with an answer.

She stood up in the meeting and told the vice president that his answer showed a lack of passion and principles. Burns' decision to speak up paid off. She and the vice president kept talking. Their conversation led to a better job for Burns, and she was on her way.

"I learned from my mother that if you have a chance to speak, you should speak," she later said in an interview. Burns said she had learned growing up on Delancey Street that if you did not speak out, "you could really be run over".

In 2009 Ursula Burns became CEO of Xerox, making her the first African-American to run a Fortune 500 company in the United States. In that role she handled tough negotiations with unions. She brought the company out of difficult financial times. And she helped engineer its transition from a copier business into a digital communications giant.

Today, Ursula Burns has retired from Xerox, but she continues to make an impact on corporate America. She is now on the board of directors of Uber, the ride-sharing company.

Sheryl Sandberg
(b. 1969)
Chief Operating Officer of Facebook

When she was growing up, Sheryl Sandberg's family valued hard work, education and helping other people. This last value, helping others, grew from an idea central to their Jewish faith: *tikkun olam*, or "repairing the world". Sandberg has described how her grandmother sold watches out of the boot of her car to raise money for the clinic that treated her breast cancer. And her parents carried on a long campaign to free persecuted Jews in the Soviet Union.

It is not surprising that helping others

is a feature of Sandberg's career. After earning a degree in economics from Harvard University in 1991, she took a job at the World Bank. She wanted to help the bank achieve its mission of decreasing global poverty. Sandberg's job was researching data, but she did have a chance to see what the numbers meant in the real world. She travelled to clinics in remote parts of India, where World Bank funds helped people suffering from the disease of leprosy.

She went back to Harvard to get an advanced degree in business. Then, in 1996, she was employed as chief of staff for the US Secretary of the Treasury. But people in political jobs such as that one are often replaced when a new president is elected. When a Republican president was elected in 2000, Sheryl decided to take a risk and join the private sector.

In 2001, she accepted a job at what

At a press conference in Paris in 2017, Sheryl Sandberg announced that Facebook would help support start-up tech companies.

was then a budding tech company called Google. And for six years, during its meteoric rise, she was vice president of global online sales and operations.

It was her next job, however, that made her a household name. Facebook's founder, Mark Zuckerberg, met her at a Christmas party in 2008. Recognizing her intelligence and drive, Zuckerberg named her chief operating officer of Facebook. Today she runs the business side of the social media company, so developers can focus on what Facebook can do for the 2 billion people who use it every month.

Carrying on her family's tradition, Sandberg has used what she learned leading Google and Facebook to help other people, especially women. Her book *Lean In* sparked a nationwide movement in the United States to help millions of women overcome the barriers preventing them acheiving the success they would like to have in business.

Indra Nooyi
(b. 1955)
CEO of PepsiCo

In the last decade Indra Nooyi has been mentioned in nearly every published list of the world's most powerful women. She is the chief executive officer of PepsiCo, the second largest food company in the world. She is responsible for more than 260,000 employees. And the company she runs generates $63.5 billion in revenue every year.

As a child, Indra was held to high standards. Her grandfather waited at the door for her monthly school report, and there would be trouble if she did not achieve the highest grades. Her mother had high expectations as well. At dinner every night, Indra and her sister regularly gave speeches about how they would change India if they were elected president or prime minister. Their mother would then announce which of them had won her vote.

After she graduated with degrees in physics, chemistry and mathematics from Madras Christian College in India,

Nooyi made a daring decision. She would leave her home in tropical southern India and pursue an advanced degree at Yale University in the United States. It was a difficult path. She worked throughout university, and once her bills were paid each month, she often had just a few dollars left.

Today, Indra Nooyi speaks to business leaders worldwide. When she talks about what it took to become CEO of a major corporation, she is honest about the obstacles she faced. She makes it clear that because she was an immigrant and a woman, her work had to be twice as good as the work of men, and those born in the United States.

Indra Nooyi, 2016

"One of the things my parents and my grandfather taught me was when you do a job you have got to do it better than everybody else," she told an interviewer. "Simple. I just don't know any other way to work."

Susan Wojcicki, 2017

Susan Wojcicki

(b. 1968)
CEO of YouTube

Two men in orange basketball shirts are lip-synching a Backstreet Boys song. They fake-wail, execute choreographed moves and, in the background, their roommate never stops doing his homework. This video is the one that convinced Susan Wojcicki that the online platform YouTube was going to be big. Millions of people all over the world were watching the lip-synching duo.

Watching YouTube's growth skyrocket was not Wojcicki's first experience with a tech start-up. Google's founders started their business in her garage in California, USA. She remembers the late night pizza-and-M&M-fuelled talks that led to the company's creation. Not only was Wojcicki their first landlord, she was Google's 16th employee.

At Google, she developed the advertising sales programmes that generate billions for the company. And she championed the deal when Google bought YouTube in 2006. Eight years later Susan became CEO at YouTube. Her aim was to increase revenue from ad sales as much as she had at Google. So far, her love of YouTube celebrities and her desire to see them succeed are doing the trick. YouTube is now worth $90 billion.

Susan is a master at making money, but she also uses her influence to change the lives of those around her. At Google, she set up the company's famous in-house creche for the children of employees. She advocated for paid maternity leave. And she uses her platform to challenge employers to employ more women in every field.

This dedication to social good may have its roots in her upbringing. She grew up on the campus of Stanford University, where her dad was a physics professor. She was surrounded by passionate scholars. She says, "Their goal wasn't to become famous or make money, it was to do something that was meaningful for the world because they had a passion."

DO WOMEN'S UNIVERSITIES PREPARE WOMEN TO LEAD?

Most students in the US and UK choose to attend co-educational universities or colleges. But are there advantages to being educated in a women-only environment? Studies show that women-only institutions educate only about 2 per cent of students, but 33 per cent of the women board members of Fortune 500 companies were educated in women-only universities. Students who attend women-only universities are also twice as likely to earn a PhD.

This image, published in Business Insider Magazine, *shows the percentage of women in leadership roles in businesses worldwide. Which figure surprises you the most?*

Source: Business Insider

Chapter 4

WOMEN WHO RULED IN MEDIA

In many ways, the women who rule in media are world-builders. They shape the way we see the world through news reporting. They create fictional worlds through art, music and fashion. Each one of these women inspires people to speak, to write and to live in a way that changes the world we share.

Katharine Graham
(1917–2001)
Publisher, *Washington Post*

Katharine Graham once said that success often came down to luck. In many ways, she was a lucky woman. Katharine was born into a wealthy family – one that operated the thriving *Washington Post* newspaper in the

Katharine Graham, 1980

United States. Yet, in some ways, she was unlucky. Men in her family viewed women as having limited abilities. When her father was ready to retire, instead of trusting the paper to Katharine, he passed it to her husband, Philip, who struggled with mental illness and was unkind to Katharine.

In 1963 Philip took his own life. Katharine felt she had three choices: sell the paper, find someone else to operate it or run it herself. Trembling, shy and terrified of public speaking, she decided to captain the paper. She was the first woman to take control of a major newspaper in the United States.

It was the first of many tough decisions she faced. In 1971 Daniel Ellsberg leaked documents that showed the government had lied about US involvement in the Vietnam War. Graham decided to publish those papers, even though the government threatened to charge her with a crime. She took the risk because she believed in the importance of a free press. Later, she and her editors decided to investigate a plot to break into Democratic Party headquarters at the Watergate Hotel. The reporting of the *Washington Post* led to the resignation of President Nixon, who was threatened with impeachment for obstruction of justice.

For its daring investigative reporting under Graham's leadership, the *Washington Post* received the Pulitzer Prize. The newspaper also became one of the most respected news sources in the world. In 1971 the paper's stock sold for $26 per share. In 1991, after 20 years of Katharine's guidance, shares sold for $222 each, an increase of more than 750 per cent.

Oprah Winfrey

(b. 1954)
Media mogul and philanthropist

When Oprah Winfrey was a child, she was dismayed by the food that came from her grandmother's garden. Eating homegrown vegetables made her feel poor. She wanted something different. Oprah was already showing a tendency that would shape her whole life: a refusal to live within the limitations others placed on her.

Oprah left rural Mississippi, USA, when she was six years old. She went to live with her mother, but she suffered extreme abuse there. She moved to Nashville, Tennessee, to live with her father. Her teenage years were sometimes troubled, but eventually she made her way to university and into a career in broadcasting.

In 1984 she began hosting a television talk show called *AM Chicago*. She was the

Oprah Winfrey attended the 2015 Film Independent Spirit Awards held at Santa Monica Beach in California, USA.

first African-American woman to host her own talk show. Shortly afterwards, it became *The Oprah Winfrey Show*. When her show was broadcast nationally in 1986, Winfrey asked her boss to give the members of her team a pay rise. He said there was no need because they were "all girls". Once again, Winfrey bristled at the unfair limitation. In 1986 she formed Harpo Productions and took control of her own show. Ratings soared. Winfrey ended her show – having been the highest-rated talk show of all time – in 2011.

Winfrey has since ventured into other fields. She acts. She produces films and Broadway musicals. In 2011, she started the Oprah Winfrey Network. During her career, she has won Emmy awards for her work in television, Academy Awards for her work in films and a Tony award for her work in theatre. In 2013 US President Obama awarded her the Presidential Medal of Freedom.

Today, Oprah Winfrey is regarded as one of the most influential people in the world. Her net financial worth is more than $2.8 billion. She has donated millions to charities worldwide, including the boarding school she established for underprivileged girls in South Africa.

J.K. Rowling
(b. 1965)
Author

Joanne Rowling grew up in England and Wales, surrounded by books. She was, she says, a classic "bookworm, complete with freckles and NHS spectacles". She began writing her own novels when she was still a child.

She penned the *Harry Potter* books when she lived in Scotland. While she worked as a teacher, she plotted and drafted the series over the course of five years, in spare moments and on scribbled scraps of paper. The manuscript of the first book, *Harry Potter and the Sorcerer's Stone*, was rejected many times, but her story finally found a home at Bloomsbury Books. When it was published in 1997, it shattered sales records in the UK, the US and across the world. Kids and adults queued up to purchase each new title in the series as it came out. The books led to films and merchandise. Eventually, they gave birth to a thriving online community of Muggle-born fans.

Harry Potter is a fantasy series, but its effects on publishing and tourism are real. Reports estimate that its popularity has led to a ten-fold increase in the number of children's books published every year. Today, children's books often outsell adult books. Potter fans flock to theme parks to experience real-life recreations of Hogwarts, Diagon Alley and Platform 9 3/4 at Kings Cross Station in London.

J.K. Rowling, 2017

In *Harry Potter and the Sorcerer's Stone*, as Harry steels himself to pass through black flames and face his enemy, he admits to his friend Hermione that she

Anna Wintour, 2017

is the better wizard. Hermione brushes off his praise.

"Me!" said Hermione. "Books! And cleverness! There are more important things . . ."

Like the witch she famously created, J.K. Rowling may credit her powers to books and cleverness. But the worlds she created in the *Harry Potter* books are magic to millions of child and adult readers all over the world.

Anna Wintour
(b. 1949)
Artistic Director, Condé Nast Publications

In each of the world's fashion capitals – Paris, London, New York, Milan – one week of the year supersedes all others. During Fashion Week, designers, models, stylists, photographers and celebrities gather to present the new clothing collections, and everyone hungers for the approval of one woman.

She arrives at the runway shows early. Her signature pageboy hair barely brushes the frames of her sunglasses. She is Dame Anna Wintour. For 30 years, she has run the world's most famous fashion magazine: *Vogue*. In its 125-year history, the magazine has never had a more influential editor than Wintour.

She is famously hands-on. As editor-in-chief, she approves colour palettes, trends, faces – every detail presented to the public. She is as fierce a guardian of the magazine's words as she is of its images. With Wintour at the helm, *Vogue's* influence on what people wear – and on what people think is beautiful – is enormous.

Wintour grew up in London in the 1960s. She stepped into the fashion world at a pivotal moment in history.

Women were entering the working world in larger numbers, earning their own money, and enjoying new personal freedoms. She put fashion and faces that celebrated this new independence on the pages of *Vogue*.

"Seeing that revolution go on made me love fashion from an early age," she said.

In 2013 Wintour expanded her influence on publishing. She was named artistic director of Condé Nast, the publishing company that owns *Vogue*. Condé Nast also owns *Vanity Fair, Glamour, The New Yorker, Architectural Digest, Bon Appétit,* and *Wired* – magazines that reach more than 120 million readers. In 2014, Wintour was made a dame in recognition of her contribution to the world of fashion. She even removed her trademark sunglasses to receive the award from the Queen.

Beyoncé Knowles, 2013

Beyoncé Knowles
(b. 1981)
Writer, Singer, Producer, Actor

From the walls of her childhood home in Houston, Texas, USA, a sisterhood of beautiful black women surrounded Beyoncé Knowles. The paintings in her mother's collection showed her what daring art looked like. It was a lesson she learned well.

Knowles began performing at the age of seven. When she was 16, she signed up to Columbia Records as part of the three-member group Destiny's Child. Their albums sold more than 60 million copies. By 2003 she had embarked on a solo career. Both commercial and critical success followed. *Rolling Stone* magazine said her vocals were "shifting the entire landscape of R&B".

But money and fame were not enough. She wanted independence. For that, she had to make a painful decision: to step out on her own, without her father as manager. Their separation caused a rift between them, but it liberated Knowles to set new goals. Her albums *4*, *Beyoncé* and *Lemonade* followed, each one achieving greater acclaim than the one before. *Lemonade,* in particular, was praised for its fierce feminism and frank critique of racism. The Formation tour that followed was criticized by some who took offence at its positive references to the Black Panthers, but many people found it empowering.

Knowles' albums have debuted six times at number one on the US Billboard charts – something no other artist has done. She has performed at the Super Bowl twice, and she sang the national anthem at the inauguration of President Obama. Her work has given rise to a $350 million empire: films, celebrity endorsements, clothing and fragrance lines, plus countless philanthropic acts.

When Knowles announced in 2016 that she was having twins, Warsan Shire wrote a poem for her entitled "I Have Three Hearts". For anyone looking at the scope, the depth and the passion of Knowles' work, that seems about right.

> *Do what you were born to do. You just have to trust yourself.*
> —Beyoncé Knowles

Chapter 5

WOMEN WHO RULED IN SPORT

These women are game changers. Each one was blessed with superior athletic talent. Each one broke records in her sport. But they did something else as well: In different ways, they opened the realm of sport to generations of young women who might otherwise have been left out.

Abby Wambach

(b. 1980)
Highest-scoring international footballer in the world

Few female footballers have amassed the titles Abby Wambach has won. World Cup Champion. Two-time Olympic gold medallist. FIFA Women's World Player of the Year in 2012. Six-time US Soccer Athlete of the Year. Highest all-time scorer on the US Women's National Team. And then there is the fact that no one, male or female, has ever scored more international goals than she has: 184 in her career.

But titles, trophies and statistics are only part of what makes this woman a champion. Her ferocity on the pitch has inspired a generation of young female

Abby Wambach during a China versus US women's match in 2015

footballers. Once, during a crucial match against Mexico in the World Cup, she leapt up to head the ball and connected instead with another player. Blood was pouring from her injured forehead, but medics stapled the wound closed, and she raced back into the match. Her intensity helped redefine what it means to play like a girl.

And she's had nearly as many victories off the pitch as she's had on. Wambach used her famously loud voice to fight for gender equality in football. She and her teammates led the drive for women's football teams to be treated the same as men's teams by FIFA, football's international governing body. When FIFA announced that important women's games would be played on AstroTurf instead of real grass, Wambach and her teammates filed a lawsuit to prevent the unfair and dangerous change in playing surface.

They fought to practise on the same quality equipment and in the same quality facilities as the men's teams. They campaigned to raise women players' salaries. Even though women's football teams won more championships, men's teams still earned more money when they lost than women's teams earned when they won. Wambach and her teammates proved that fierce advocacy works. In 2017 the US Women's football team negotiated a contract that dramatically increased their pay and improved their working conditions.

Scoring 184 international goals is a stunning accomplishment. But her campaign to empower girls and women in the sport may outlast her scoring record. She taught girls and young women to pursue their goals with relentless ferocity, both on and off the pitch.

Misty Copeland

(b. 1980)
Principal dancer,
American Ballet Theatre

Some people are born into wealth and that can make rising to greatness easier. That was not the case for Misty Copeland. When she was a child, her mother worked hard but struggled to earn enough to take care of Misty and her five siblings. Sometimes there were no beds to sleep in. Sometimes they bought food with coins they found under the sofa cushions. But Misty had gifts of another kind. She had an amazing talent for dancing.

Her natural ability was spotted by a volunteer dance teacher at the Boys & Girls Club in her neighbourhood. Misty started dancing when she was 13, years later than most professional dancers. But she picked up movements quickly. She was as flexible as a pipe cleaner. And

Misty Copeland, 2015

she spent hours practising. *Plié. Tendu. Battement.* Every sweep of her slipper built strength, precision and grace.

The instructor at the Boys & Girls Club offered Copeland classes at a private studio. She invited Copeland to live in her home so she could focus on dance. From there, Copeland's determination and talent opened one door after another, from San Francisco Ballet to the American Ballet Theatre's summer intensive programme. Then she studied at the American Ballet Theatre's studio company. And after that, a position in the American Ballet Theatre's corps de ballet. She danced every coveted role in classical ballet – Clara in *The Nutcracker*, Odette in *Swan Lake*, Juliet in *Romeo & Juliet* – and many times she was the first African-American woman to do so. There were times when people told her she had grown too curvy to dance those classical roles. There were times she was desperately lonely as the only African-American female in the company. There were times she was prevented from dancing because of injury. But she persevered. *Plié. Tendu. Battement.*

In 2015 Misty Copeland was promoted to principal dancer in the American Ballet Theatre. She is the first black woman ever to rise to that position in the company. Her presence on stage, dancing these coveted roles, shows African-American girls that ballet is for everyone.

Pat Summitt
(1952–2016)
College basketball coach

Some of the most influential people in sport are the coaches that bring out the greatness in others. Pat Summitt is one of those people in the history of basketball.

She has been described as a hurricane: a force of nature that drove teams to victory. In her 38-year coaching career, Summitt never had a losing season. She won 1,098 games, more than any other NCAA Division I basketball coach, male or female. She led her teams to eight NCAA national championships, the most for any women's basketball coach in history. She won National Coach of the Year seven times.

And Pat was a fierce athlete herself. She won an Olympic silver medal in 1976, the first time women's basketball was played as an Olympic sport. Eight years later, she coached the US team that won gold.

Though she was renowned for her steely glare and fierce tactics, Summitt was loved with equal ferocity. In 2011, she was diagnosed with dementia, a disease that affects a person's ability to remember. Near the end of her life, former players came from across the United States to sit by her bedside. One of them, Sheila Collins, brought a letter Summitt had written to her before her first game. It read:

Winning is fun … Sure.

But winning is not the point.

Pat Summitt, 2012

Wanting to win is the point.

Not giving up is the point.

Never letting up is the point.

Never being satisfied with what you've done is the point.

The game is never over. No matter what the scoreboard reads, or what the referee says, it doesn't end when you come off the court.

In 2012 US President Obama awarded Summitt the nation's highest civilian honour: the Presidential Medal of Freedom.

Summitt's contribution to women's sport did not end when she left the court. It is a mark of her profound influence on basketball that more than 75 of her former players have gone on to become coaches themselves, passing the ball to future generations.

Wilma Rudolph
(1940–1994)
Olympic sprinter and civil rights activist

Wilma Rudolph was outrunning adversity from day one. She was born early, weighing little more than 1.8 kilograms (4 pounds). The nearest hospital refused to take care of Wilma and her mother because they were black. As a result, Wilma Rudolph fell ill and contracted polio.

Her doctor said she would never walk. But Wilma's mother insisted that she would, and Wilma believed her. She took off her leg brace by herself. She let her family members massage the leg that had been twisted by polio. By the age of 6 she was hopping around the house. By 11 she was playing basketball barefoot.

Well-known athletics coach Ed Temple noticed Rudolph's talent and began to train her. She ran in university track and field events though she was only at high school.

When Rudolph was 16 she competed in the 1956 Olympics in Melbourne, Australia. She won a bronze medal in the 400-metre relay. In 1960 she competed at the Rome Olympics. This time, she went home with three medals – all of them gold. She also broke three world records. Rudolph was being called "the fastest woman in the world".

When she returned to Tennessee, she faced the same racism that had resulted in

Wilma Rudolph is shown holding up the three gold medals she won at the 1960 Olympics in Rome.

her contracting polio earlier in her life. The parade planned in her honour would be segregated – no African Americans would be allowed to attend. Rudolph got angry.

She refused to attend – and her protest worked. Her welcome home parade was the first integrated event in her town's history.

In 1983 Rudolph was inducted into the Olympic Hall of Fame. Historian Bud Greenspan said she had changed the world of sport forever.

Serena Williams
(b. 1981)
Champion tennis player

Serena Williams and her sister Venus grew up in Compton, a poor neighbourhood in California, USA, troubled by violence and drug use. But the Williams family had big aspirations for Venus and Serena. Venus says that at eight years old, she announced the intention to win Wimbledon five times (she achieved that goal in 2008). Serena played extra hard because she felt she was a "runt". The skills she learned helped compensate for her smaller size.

Serena Williams has won 23 Grand Slam titles in 29 singles matches, more than any other player – male or female – in the open era. She has won four Olympic gold medals, including three she shares with her sister Venus for doubles matches. Serena has earned nearly $85 million in prize money and has more than twelve endorsement partners.

Her generosity is equally admirable. Serena has started schools in Kenya and Jamaica. She works with schools in Compton to keep them stocked with equipment. She established the Yetunde Price Resource Centre, named after her older sister, Yetunde, who died as a result of gun violence. The centre offers help to those recovering from the effects of violence in their community.

Williams is a bold advocate for women everywhere. She said, "The cycles of poverty, discrimination and sexism are much, much harder to break than the record for Grand Slam titles."

Serena Williams, 2016

Serena Williams has frequently held the top spot in her sport over the years. She has won more matches than anyone else in professional tennis. Her physical strength, the pinpoint accuracy of her serves and the ferocious speed at which she propels a ball mean that she rules the court. And she rose to that position over obstacles that could have crushed a weaker person: race, money, gender. None of them was a match for her. And for those reasons, many people say Serena Williams is the best athlete of all time.

Timeline

1910 Elizabeth Arden opens her beauty salon

1912 15,000 suffragettes march in the streets of New York City

1953 Elizabeth II becomes queen

1963 Katharine Graham becomes President of the *Washington Post*

1966 Indira Gandhi becomes the first female prime minister of India

1968 Shirley Chisholm is elected to United States Congress

1972 Shirley Chisholm announces she is running for the United States Presidency

1976 Pat Summitt wins an Olympic silver medal in basketball

1979 Margaret Thatcher becomes Prime Minister of the UK

1981 Sandra Day O'Connor becomes the first woman appointed to the US Supreme Court

1984 Brenda Hale becomes first woman appointed to the Law Commission

1986 The Oprah Winfrey Show debuts

1988 Benazir Bhutto begins first term as Prime Minister of Pakistan

1990 Margaret Thatcher resigns as Prime Minister of the UK

1993 Benazir Bhutto begins second term as Prime Minister of Pakistan

1996 Madeleine Albright is confirmed as United States Secretary of State

1997 J.K. Rowling publishes her first *Harry Potter* book

2000 Michelle Bachelet becomes Minister of Health in Chile

2001 Sheryl Sandberg joins Google

2002 Michelle Bachelet becomes Minister of National Defence in Chile

2005 Angela Merkel is elected chancellor of Germany

2005 Ellen Johnson Sirleaf becomes President of Liberia

2006 Michelle Bachelet begins first term as President of Chile

2006 Indra Nooyi becomes President and CEO of PepsiCo

2008 Sheryl Sandberg named chief operating officer of Facebook

2009 Brenda Hale becomes first woman ever appointed to Supreme Court of the United Kingdom

2009 Ursula Burns becomes CEO of Xerox

2010 Michelle Bachelet ends first term as President of Chile

2011 Ellen Johnson Sirleaf awarded Nobel Peace Prize

2012 Madeleine Albright is awarded the Presidential Medal of Freedom

2012 Abby Wambach is named FIFA Women's World Player of the Year

2012 Pat Summitt is awarded the Presidential Medal of Freedom

2013 Michelle Bachelet begins second term as President of Chile

2013 Anna Wintour becomes artistic director of Condé Nast

2014 Susan Wojcicki becomes CEO of YouTube

2015 Misty Copeland is promoted to principal dancer in the American Ballet Theatre

2016 Beyoncé's album *Lemonade* is released

2016 Serena Williams wins her seventh Wimbeldon title

2017 Michelle Bachelet ends second term as President of Chile

2017 The US Women's football team negotiates a contract that increases their pay and improves working conditions

Glossary

advocacy recommending an action publicly

assassinate murder a leader for political or religious reasons

ceremony special actions, words or music performed to mark an important event

concentration camp camp where people such as prisoners of war, political prisoners or refugees are held

Congress national legislative body of the United States

corps de ballet group of primary performers in a ballet company

coup violent change in the leadership of a government, often by the military

coveted something that many people would like to have

democratic government in which the citizens elect their leaders

endorsement to do with marketing and selling a product

gender cultural or social behaviours associated with masculinity or femininity

impeachment charging a high-ranking person, such as a president, with a crime that means they are unfit for office

indigenous native to a place

persecute punish or treat badly for one's beliefs

recession temporary slowing of business activity

refugee person who flees his or her homeland because of oppression or disaster

Comprehension questions

1. The author of this book used autobiographies and interviews with the women featured. What are some of the advantages of using these sources? What are the disadvantages of relying on the stories a person tells about her own life?
2. Compare the backgrounds of the women in this book. With such different life stories, what characteristics do these women share?
3. Modern culture supports male leaders being ambitious, assertive and confident. When women display the same characteristics, they are seen differently. Why do you think this is the case? What might change that? How could changing our language habits encourage more girls to want to become leaders?

Find out more

Books

Amazing Women: Discover Inspiring Life Stories, Caryn Jenner (DK Children, 2017)

Angela Merkel (Extraordinary Women), Claire Throp (Raintree, 2014)

Benazir Bhutto (Front-Page Lives), Sean Price (Raintree, 2010)

Queen Elizabeth II and the Royal Family: A Glorious Illustrated History, DK (DK, 2016)

Stories of Women in the 1960s: Fighting for Freedom (Women's Stories from History), Cath Senker (Raintree, 2016)

Websites

Learn more about Queen Elizabeth II at:
www.bbc.co.uk/schools/primaryhistory/famouspeople/elizabeth_ii/

Source notes

Pages 6–8: Chris Leadbeater. "The Queen's 90 Years – and 271 Foreign Trips." *Telegraph*. June 13, 2016, http://www.telegraph.co.uk/travel/news/Around-the-world-with-the-Queen/

Pages 8–10:
Karl Vick. "TIME Person of the Year 2015: Angela Merkel." *TIME*. http://time.com/time-person-of-the-year-2015-angela-merkel/

"The Reunification of Germany." Encyclopedia Britannica. May 2, 2018, https://www.britannica.com/place/Germany/The-reunification-of-Germany

Pages 14–15:
Jason Burke. "Benazir Bhutto." *The Guardian*. December 27, 2007, https://www.theguardian.com/world/2007/dec/28/pakistan.obituaries

Jane Perlez and Victoria Burnett. "Benazir Bhutto, 54, Lived in Eye of Pakistan Storm." *The New York Times*. December 28, 2007, http://www.nytimes.com/2007/12/28/world/asia/28bhuttocnd.html

Pages 16–19:
Afua Hirsch. "Can Ellen Johnson Sirleaf Save Liberia?" *The Guardian*. 22 July 2017. https://www.theguardian.com/global-development/2017/jul/23/can-president-ellen-johnson-sirleaf-save-liberia

"Ellen Johnson Sirleaf — Facts." Nobel Prize Organization. https://www.nobelprize.org/nobel_prizes/peace/laureates/2011/johnson_sirleaf-facts.html

Pages 19–21:
Larry Rohter. "Chile Inagurates First Woman to Serve as Its President." *The New York Times*. March 12, 2006, http://www.nytimes.com/2006/03/12/world/americas/chile-inaugurates-first-woman-to-serve-as-its-president.html

"Chilean President Speaks of her Torture Under Pinochet." Yahoo. November 14, 2014, https://www.yahoo.com/news/chilean-president-speaks-her-torture-under-pinochet-192814454.html

Pages 23-25:
"Shirley Chisholm Biography." Biography. https://www.biography.com/people/shirley-chisholm-9247015

"Shirley Chisholm, Pioneer in Congress, Dies at 80." NBC News. January 4, 2005, http://www.nbcnews.com/id/6779424/#.VUUPjPlViko

Pages 25–26:
"Baroness Hale Appointed as UK's First Female Top Judge." *BBC.* July 21, 2017, http://www.bbc.com/news/uk-40679293

Clare Dyer. "The Guardian Profile: Lady Brenda Hale." *The Guardian.* January 9, 2004, https://www.theguardian.com/uk/2004/jan/09/lords.women

Pages 28–30: Faith Dallal. "100 Years Behind the Iconic Red Door." *Vanity Fair.* November 8, 2010, https://www.vanityfair.com/style/2010/11/100-years-behind-the-iconic-red-door

Pages 30–32:
Kathleen Elkins. "How Calling Out a VP Helped an Entry-Level Employee Become CEO of Xerox." CNBC. February 7, 2017, https://www.cnbc.com/2017/02/07/calling-out-a-vp-helped-an-entry-level-employee-become-ceo-of-xerox.html

"Ursula Burns: CEO, Xerox Corporation." Makers. https://www.makers.com/profiles/591f28b1bea177748042171a

Pages 34–35: "Indra Nooyi." Encyclopedia Britannica. November 22, 2017, https://www.britannica.com/biography/Indra-Nooyi

Pages 51–52: "Discover Misty's Journey." The Official Website of Misty Copeland. http://mistycopeland.com/about/

Pages 52–54:
Sally Jenkins. "'The Game is Never Over': A Letter from Pat Summitt to a Young Basketball Player." *The Washington Post.* June 28, 2016, https://www.washingtonpost.com/sports/colleges/widely-beloved-pat-summitt-was-cherished-most-by-those-who-saw-her-complexities/2016/06/28/581a391a-3d2e-11e6-80bc-d06711fd2125_story.html?tid=a_inl&utm_term=.9fbe7df82476

Gary Smith. "Eyes of the Storm." *Sports Illustrated.* Mar 2, 1998, https://www.si.com/vault/1998/03/02/239460/eyes-of-the-storm-when-tennessees-whirlwind-of-a-coach-pat-summitt-hits-you-with-her-steely-gaze-you-get-a-dose-of-the-intensity-that-has-carried-the-lady-vols-to-five-ncaa-titles

Pages 54–56:
KeriLynn Engel. "Wilma Rudolph, Olympic Gold Medalist & Civil Rights Pioneer." Amazing Women in History. August 14, 2012, http://www.amazingwomeninhistory.com/wilma-rudolph-olympic-gold-medalist-civil-right-pioneer/

Frank Litsky. "Wilma Rudolph, Star of the 1960 Olympics, Dies at 54." *The New York Times.* 1994. http://www.nytimes.com/1994/11/13/obituaries/wilma-rudolph-star-of-the-1960-olympics-dies-at-54.html

Barbara Heilman. "Like Nothing Else in Tennessee." *Sports Illustrated.* November 14, 1960, https://www.si.com/vault/1960/11/14/585203/like-nothing-else-in-tennessee

Select bibliography

Bedell Smith, Sally. *Elizabeth the Queen*. New York: Random House, 2012.

Bhutto, Benazir. *Daughter of Destiny*. New York: Harper Collins, 2008.

Chisholm, Shirley. *Unbought & Unbossed*. Ontario, Canada: Take Root Media Edition, 2010.

Copeland, Misty and Charisse Jones. *Life in Motion*. New York: Scholastic, Inc., 2014.

Johnson Sirleaf, Ellen. *This Child Will Be Great*. New York: Harper Perennial, 2009.

Malhotra, Inder. *Indira Gandhi, A Personal and Political Biography*. Boston, Mass.: Northeastern University Press, 2012.

Muñoz, Heraldo. *Getting Away With Murder: Benazir Bhutto's Assassination and the Politics of Pakistan*. New York: W. W. Norton & Company, 2013.

Qvortrup, Matthew. *Angela Merkel: Europe's Most Influential Leader*. New York: Overlook Duckworth, 2016.

Thatcher, Margaret. *The Autobiography*. New York: Harper Perennial, 2013.

Wambach, Abby. *Forward*. New York: Harper Collins, 2016.

Winfrey, Oprah. *What I Know for Sure*. New York: Flatiron Books, 2014.

Woodhead, Lindy. *War Paint*. Hoboken, N.J.: Wiley, 2008.

About the author

Rebecca Stanborough obtained her BA from Agnes Scott College, a women's college in Georgia, USA. She also earned an MFA in Writing for Children and Adults from Minnesota's Hamline University. Rebecca is the author of four other books for young readers, and her short story "The Latter Days of Jean" appeared in the Capstone anthology *Love & Profanity*. She writes and teaches in Florida, USA.

Index